When Trauma Writes The Story Triumph Wins!

——— FROM ———
BROKENNESS
TO BEAUTY

I0117152

BOOK FOUR

Dr. Kayla Bullard

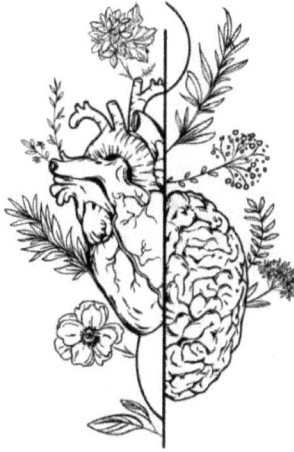

FROM BROKENNESS TO BEAUTY

ISBN: 979-8-9927612-3-8
Published by:

OWL®
PUBLISHERS

www.owlpublishers.com

360 S Market St, San Jose, CA 95113,
United States.
Printed in the United States of America

DEDICATION

To every silent sufferer,
the ones whose pain was buried under shame,
whose voices were stolen by trauma,
and whose identities were distorted by what was done to
them:
this book is for you.

You are not forgotten.
You are not too far gone.
And you are not alone.

May these pages become a safe place for your healing to
begin,
a reminder that Jesus sees you, knows you,
and loves you beyond measure.

To the wounded, the weary, and the rising,
may you find beauty in the ashes,
freedom in the truth,
and wholeness in the arms of your Healer.

FORWARD

Endorsed & Scripted by Yahweh!

"מוסמך ומבושל על ידי יהוה!"

PREFACE

There are some stories we never planned to tell. Some wounds feel too deep, too personal, or too painful to bring into the light. For many, sexual abuse is one of those stories hidden behind closed doors, buried under silence, or carried with unshed tears. But silence doesn't bring healing; truth does. And it is through truth, brought into the presence of Jesus Christ, that shame becomes beauty.

This book was born out of a deep burden for the men and women who carry unseen wounds, for the believers who love God but wrestle with shame, and for the Church that has, for too long, struggled to find the words to address sexual trauma and sin with both grace and truth. The pages that follow are not written from a place of judgment, but from a place of mercy. They are not just theological insights or psychological frameworks; they are invitations into healing encounters with the Healer Himself.

Within these chapters, you will find the stories of pain, yes, but also stories of hope, redemption, and triumph. You will see biblical examples of shame and witness how God restored what seemed beyond repair. And you will be gently led through the process of acknowledging wounds, confronting lies, reclaiming identity, and receiving the healing that only Jesus can give.

Whether you are a survivor, someone seeking freedom from your own past choices, or a compassionate guide walking alongside others, this book is for you. My prayer is that these words will serve as a mirror, ointment, and a map. A mirror to reflect the truth of where you are. An ointment to soothe the wounds you carry. And a map to guide you toward the wholeness your soul has been longing for.

Healing is possible. Freedom is real. And with Christ, the story doesn't end in shame. It ends in victory.

From Trauma to Triumph!

Table of Content

INTRODUCTION

This is a book about wounds, and the God who heals them. Across generations and cultures, countless people carry deep, hidden pain rooted in sexual shame. Some wounds are the result of choices made in moments of weakness. Others are inflicted without consent, leaving behind invisible scars that shape how we see ourselves, how we trust, and how we live. Whether you're the one who caused harm or the one who was harmed, one truth remains: pain demands healing.

Meet **Charlie**: A quiet, intelligent teenage boy who walked through life carrying a secret too heavy for his young shoulders. Abused by someone he should have been able to trust, Charlie bore the shame and confusion of sexual trauma in silence. Outwardly, he smiled. Inwardly, he crumbled. Guilt haunted him. Fear silenced him. His sense of identity warped under the weight of what was never his fault. For years, he believed he was too broken to be whole again, until he encountered the healing presence of Jesus Christ.

Now meet **King David**, one of the most prominent figures in the Bible. A man after God's own heart, yet deeply flawed. In a moment of lust and power, David took another man's wife, then orchestrated a cover-up soaked in blood. His fall was steep. His remorse was real. And yet, through the piercing words of the prophet Nathan, David was brought to his knees, not in shame, but in repentance. And in that sacred place of surrender, he found mercy. Redemption. Restoration.

Charlie and David come from very different places: one a victim, the other an offender. However, their stories intersect at the same crossroads - shame and a desperate need for healing. Both had to face truth. Both had to let go of the lies. Both had to surrender. And both encountered a God who does not shy away from the messiness of human pain. They were met, not with condemnation, but with a love that runs deeper than the wound.

This book isn't just about them; it's about *you*. About the parts of your story that feel too damaged, too complicated, or too shameful to speak out loud. It's about the healing that Jesus offers to every person who dares to bring their shame into His light.

You will find in these pages the truth of Scripture, the reality of pain, and the hope of redemption. Whether you carry the weight of trauma like Charlie, the burden of guilt like David, or a silent storm all your own, you are not beyond God's reach.

This is more than a book. It is a refuge for the wounded. A sacred invitation to breathe again, to believe again, to begin again. Let this moment mark the turning of the page in your life's story, not into more silence, but into healing. Not into more shame, but into purpose. Not into hiding, but into holy restoration.

Here, your pain finds a voice. Your wounds become wisdom. And your shame becomes the canvas for God's masterpiece.

This is not the end of your story.

With Christ, shame is never the final word.
Redemption is.
Wholeness is.
Triumph is.

CHAPTER ONE

I could not believe we did it; nor had I anticipated the fallout. The sirens blared. The emergency valves sprayed a special solution and water over the chemistry lab. My lab group, unbeknownst to the teacher, had just created our first hydrogen explosion. The eruption felt exhilarating, yet terrifying.

The blast threw me to the floor, and as I struggled to recover, I noticed the absence of my classmates. They had already evacuated, filing out through the emergency exit to the safe zone as designated by the evacuation protocol. With my heart pounding and adrenaline coursing through my veins, I staggered to my feet and stumbled toward the nearest emergency exit. As I rushed through the empty corridors, the sound of distant alarms served as a haunting reminder of the danger I had purposefully created.

I could hear the commotion in the distance, but the ringing in my ears muffled all the surrounding sounds. My eardrum felt tender, with a deep, pulsing ache. I could make out voices, but their words were indistinguishable. Panic dulled the sensation in my right ear. Through the haze, I saw safety monitors in neon vests stationed at the exit doors.

Amidst the shattered glass and scattered debris, students were being quietly evacuated and directed away from the science block to safety. An extreme rush of adrenaline surged through me. I almost wished I had died in the blast. Fear and anxiety took over, steering me away from the evacuation zone. Instead, I darted to the student parking lot and headed for the bicycle racks.

In record time, I hopped on my motorized bike and sped home, passing two fire trucks racing to mitigate the disaster at

Oak Ridge High School. What was usually a 30-minute ride took me less than 15 minutes. For the first time in months, I craved the privacy of my room. I needed to erase any trace of this incident from my school-issued laptop. As I neared home, I prayed loudly that Candace was not there.

Turning the corner toward my house, I saw a beautiful sight: a fire-red, 18-foot trailer parked across our driveway. My heart skipped a beat. Could it be my dad? He had been gone for two months, the longest trip he had ever taken. He worked tirelessly as a semi-truck driver. He often promised that once he had his truck, he would not have to drive as much and would be home more often.

My heart skipped two consecutive beats. I missed my dad. I longed for the day when he would finally be home, his presence filling the empty spaces in our house. The sound of his laughter and the warmth of his embrace were cherished memories I held onto tightly.

I missed my friend. Throwing my bike down, I sprinted the last fifty yards to the front door. It was unlocked, and I burst inside with exuberance and excitement, eager to celebrate my father's success. Overjoyed, I hoped for his reassuring hug. But my feelings were short-lived.

When I got inside, helium balloons were everywhere, filling the lofty ceilings. A kaleidoscope of colors intersected the open foyer. Red, white, green, yellow, orange, and blue confetti draped the furniture. The party was in full swing, and I had not been invited. The curiosity poked me in the gut, and it quickly turned to shame and guilt.

I heard the familiar sounds of laughter and erotic squealing. Candace, my stepmother, was at work. The '90s tunes blasted as she rode the bull. She was expressing her enjoyment as she lewdly pranced up and down. She was reenacting her days as a rodeo star. I knew her sounds all too well. The musty scent of her arousal assaulted the air. I spun around like the devil was at the back of my heels, and I ran, grabbing a bottle of water from a nearby table, slamming the door in desperation.

Hyperventilating, I clutched my chest as I felt the tightening of my right ventricle restricting the flow of blood to my heart. Despite the pressure in my chest, I willed my mind and feet to respond. I ran until I was spent. I did not have a destination; I just had to get away. I ended up in the cemetery and searched until I found the weather-beaten headstone that marked my mother's grave.

I cried and lamented, "Mother, why did you leave? Mother, I need you. Mother, come back." The pain is too great. I can no longer bear it. I collapsed to my knees, the weight of my grief crushing me. Tears poured down my face as I whispered, "I miss you so much, Mom. Life isn't the same without you." I stayed there, lost in a sea of memories, hoping to somehow feel her presence once more.

As I clung to the cold stone, I was overcome with a profound sense of loss. I let out a deep sigh, trying to gather my thoughts and find solace in the stillness of the cemetery. The wind whispered through the trees as if carrying her words of comfort from beyond. I closed my eyes, allowing the wind to caress my face, imagining it was my mother's gentle touch.

After hours of unrestrained hollering and bitter lamenting, exhaustion finally overtook me, and I slept for what felt like an eternity. Waves of taunting memories flooded my mind. Before my mother passed away, I was a happy child. My dad was my hero and savior. We spent hours talking, playing video games, and engaging in sports like basketball, football, and baseball. We even enjoyed swimming, fishing, and riding my dirt bike together with my mom. We did so much together, but after Mom's death, he withdrew. With her gone, my father lost a part of himself. Laughter and joy vanished, replaced by a heavy silence that hung over us.

Time seemed to stand still. Until one day, I returned home from school and Dad was casually introducing me to Candace, my new mother. It was an ordinary day, with nothing exciting except for homemade spaghetti and freshly baked garlic bread instead of our usual canned soup. It was my first home-cooked meal in a long time, and it tasted just like Mom's. That weekend, we played card games and watched Netflix together.

CHAPTER TWO

A few days later, Dad left to transport a shipment to Alaska. He said goodbye after breakfast and handed me a pocketful of bills for my allowance. He urged me to manage them well since he was not sure when he would return. He had to work hard to pay off some pressing loans. Candace kept to herself, and I focused on school, spending most of my time in my room.

Thursday's track practice was grueling, worsened by days of consecutive rain that had left the ground soaked and soggy. Instead of the usual 5-mile terrain, the coach added two additional miles that day. The team huddled together, drenched in sweat and rain, as the coach explained the importance of mental toughness in adverse weather conditions. Despite the challenge, I felt a surge of determination to push through and improve my endurance.

Cross-country running was my escape, a way to release pent-up emotions. Despite physical and mental fatigue, I pushed through the soggy terrain that felt like weights on my legs. I ran alone, completing the task at record speed, rushing home before threatening storm clouds gathered. I despised thunderstorms and deeply missed my mother's comforting embrace; I longed for her presence to soothe my fears. She used to console me with warm milk on scary nights and sing me to sleep. Her voice would drift through the air, enveloping my room with a sense of security and solace. Those memories wrapped around me like a soft blanket, offering some respite from the storm raging outside.

After a quick shower, I fell asleep immediately. A loud crashing of thunder woke me from my slumber. I rolled over to go to the bathroom, but I was restricted. I could not move; my feet were bound, and my hands were tied above my head.

Screaming was useless because a thick ward of duct tape was plastered across my mouth and nose, allowing me only a minuscule space to breathe without suffocating. Bewildered, my dilated pupils adjusted to the dark room, and I saw Candace in the corner, watching intensely, urging me to open my eyes.

My heart raced as I struggled to comprehend the situation, feeling a surge of panic and fear coursing through my veins. I strained against the restraints, trying to form words with my eyes to communicate with Candace. But the dim light in the room made it hard for me to clearly see her. I could feel the adrenaline pumping through my body as I desperately tried to find a way to escape. The sound of my pounding heart filled my ears as I searched for a way out of the tight, coarse ropes. Panic overpowered me as I realized the magnitude of my situation.

Candace's favorite tunes were playing in the background. She approached me, speaking softly. I could not hear what she was saying. Focusing on her, I watched her sway to the music as the hypnotic rhythm of her hips caused my lower body to burn. She advanced towards me, whispering and smiling at her conquest. Bowing low, she approached and began to caress my legs, arms, and chest. My body betrayed me and responded to her massages. Her touch was electrifying, sending shivers down my spine and awakening a desire I had never felt before.

As she continued to explore my body, I surrendered to the intoxicating sensation, losing myself in the depths of her seduction. Every touch ignited a fire within me, consuming all rational thoughts and leaving only raw passion in its wake. My senses were overwhelmed as she traced her fingers back and forth along my skin.

Leaving a trail of burning desire, I felt emotions that I had never before experienced in my fifteen years. My lower member stood at attention. Candace adjusted my body and rotated me to a perpendicular position on the bed. She mounted like a horse and rocked until she was spent.

Her seductive movements ignited a fire deep within, leaving me helpless and confused, swept into a whirlwind of conflicting emotions. That night marked the beginning of countless others, where I felt trapped, manipulated, and violated. The emotional devastation of being raped was unbearable. Each nighttime visit robbed me of sleep, leaving me mentally and emotionally exhausted and irritable during the day. I was eager for my dad to come home; I needed to tell him everything. But the fear of not being believed paralyzed me into silence.

The mounting pressure weighed heavily on me, making me question my very existence. I wasn't sure how much longer I could endure the painful silence.

Somehow, confessing to my father became an elusive wish because I kept missing his visits. I knew he came home in my absence because the tell-tale signs of his presence were clear: money and notes left behind. Yet, he was always gone before I woke up or returned from school. His signature scent of Esteban Cuban cigar filled the house, and ashes on the front steps were evidence that he had been there.

The lingering aroma of his favorite cigar haunted the rooms of our home, a constant signature of his elusive visits. No matter how hard I tried to catch him, he always managed to slip away, leaving me with unanswered questions and a sense of loneliness. As I walked through the empty hallways of my house, I could not help but experience constant waves of sadness. The memories we had created together whispered to me from every corner, reminding me of his absence and the void in my broken heart.

Candace no longer restricted my body during her nightly escapades. Once unbound, my hands were free to roam. The days passed in robotic participation, as I urged my body not to respond to Candace's manipulations. She knew how to ignite the fires within me. Her rhythmic melodies captured my attention, and like the pied piper, my body responded obediently. Merciless, she did not cease until she achieved release, bringing me repeatedly to shameful moments of ecstasy. Blaming me for her sins, she accused me relentlessly of tempting and ensnaring her into her descent into sexual madness.

Despite each accusation and twisted manipulation, I mustered the strength to keep getting up and going to school, which put me out of her destructive grasp for precious hours. Filled with disgust, my haven was short-lived because the weight of her toxicity followed and tainted the air around me even as I stepped foot into the classroom. The place I had hoped to find solace from her twisted web of deceit was polluted by the tangled emotional web she had spun.

The unexpected sound of birds chirping nearby startled me back into awareness. A flock, hidden somewhere in the trees, broke the silence with their bright, oblivious song; life moving on all around me. That's when I noticed the dull ache in my left side. My arm had gone numb beneath me, a quiet protest from lying too long in an unnatural position. I was stretched out across the cold, unyielding slab of my mother's grave. But at that moment, I didn't care. Oblivious to the discomfort, I had pressed myself close to the stone as if the nearness could bring her back. My body reaching for something my heart still couldn't let go of. There, in the stillness, with my cheek against etched granite, I had felt a strange, aching comfort as if the cold could hold me in the ways she no longer could. But now, consciousness had returned, and with it, pain. The realization that I couldn't stay. I would have to get up. I would have to leave and return home.

As the flood of memories slowly receded, I lay there, mentally drained, bitter, and exhausted, folded across her tombstone like a child clinging to what little remained. I cursed my helplessness, the way grief held me captive, but I didn't move. I couldn't. My emotions spilled silently; wordless prayers arose from my soul as I watched the sun retreat behind the horizon.

Tears ran freely, unrestrained, as if my body could no longer hold the weight of sorrow. And beneath the widening sky, as twilight deepened and the first stars began to shimmer above, I wished desperately for release, for some kind of peace.

I remained there a while longer, still and aching beneath the open sky, until the last trace of light slipped beneath the horizon. Then, almost like a thread being pulled through the silence, came the gentle rise of melodious worship music drifting through the air. The voices were faint, softened by distance, but unmistakably warm, familiar harmonies carried on the breeze like an invitation. Alongside it came another unexpected comfort: the rich, smoky scent of a country BBQ pit. It was jarring, almost surreal, grief and hunger coexisting in the same moment. My stomach growled, reminding me that it had been hours since I'd eaten, though I hadn't noticed until now.

Wiping the tear stains from my face with the sleeve of my shirt, I slowly pushed myself up from the cold stone. My limbs protested, heavy and stiff, but something was shifting inside me, small, subtle. Life was still moving.

People were singing. Food was being prepared. The world, in its quiet way, was reminding me that I was still part of it. The music and the scent seemed to be coming from nearby, Emmanuel Baptist Fellowship Church, if I had to guess.

The name alone stirred something in me. **Emmanuel. God with us.** Maybe I didn't feel Him yet. Perhaps I wasn't sure I believed He was here. But something about that name made me pause. And so, with a heart still sore and eyes still burning, I let the sound and scent guide me forward. Not because I was ready, but because something in me refused to stay frozen at the edge of that grave.

The small, quaint structure came into view, nestled between the edge of the graveyard and the still waters of the lake, its silhouette outlined by the soft glow of evening lights.

Emmanuel Baptist Fellowship Church. I recognized it now. This was the place, humble and weathered, where summer revivals had been held for as long as I could remember. I had only been inside once or twice, but I recalled my mom talking about it often. She'd come here once in her final months, moved by something she couldn't fully explain at the time. I hadn't thought much of it then. But now, as I drew closer, the sound of the hymn grew clearer. Familiar chords rose and fell through the open windows, carried on the air like a whisper meant just for me.

And then I heard it. A melody I hadn't realized I still remembered, *"It Is Well with My Soul."* My feet slowed, heart quickening in contrast. My mother loved that hymn. She used to sing softly while folding laundry, stirring soup, or driving with the windows down. Hearing it now, drifting out of that little church by the water, felt like stepping into a memory wrapped in warmth and ache.

The notes filled my chest, swelling with something I couldn't quite name, nostalgia, maybe. Or grace. Or the echo of a voice I would never hear again, yet somehow still lived on inside me.

A lump rose in my throat as the memory overtook me: my mother's voice, steady and gentle, singing those words not just as a song, but as a declaration. *"Whatever my lot, thou hast taught me to say..."* I blinked hard, feeling the sting behind my eyes return. A fresh wave of emotion crashed over me. Grief, yes, but also something tenderer, a trace of comfort, of being known.

Without thinking, I quickened my pace; drawn not just by the music or the smell of barbecue, but by the chance, however fragile, to feel close to her again. To step inside a place she once cherished. To follow her footsteps, maybe even to meet the God she had clung to when everything else was slipping away.

CHAPTER THREE

As I neared the picnic benches, the scent of smoked meat and warm bread wrapped around me like a blanket I hadn't known I needed. A man stood at the serving table, older, with kind eyes and weathered hands. He didn't say a word, just met my gaze and offered a quiet smile before handing me a plate.

Without asking, he began to fill it with slow, deliberate motions. A generous portion of brisket, steaming corn-on-the-cob, baked beans rich with molasses, and a soft dinner roll still warm from the oven. Then he pressed a cold glass of sweet tea into my free hand, beads of condensation already forming on the sides.

I ate without speaking; my hunger was more voracious than I realized. Each bite grounded me; something about the simplicity of the meal, the unspoken grace in being fed. When my plate was empty, he refilled it. Same with the tea. No words passed between us, but something passed, nonetheless.

When I finally leaned back, full for the first time that day, I offered him a small, grateful smile. He returned it with a knowing nod, like he understood more than I'd said. Then, without breaking his quiet rhythm, he lifted a hand and gently gestured toward the church, where the music still floated through the air like an invitation.

Drawn by the music, I followed its pull across the lawn until I reached a large white alfresco tent, glowing under strings of hanging lights. It was overflowing with locals; men, women, children, all gathered shoulder to shoulder on folding chairs and picnic blankets, their eyes fixed forward. I lingered at the edge, unsure whether I belonged, but too captivated to turn away.

FROM BROKENNESS TO BEAUTY

The moment I stepped beneath the tent's cover, the hum of voices fell away. A single voice filled the space, clear, rich, and commanding. The singer was an elderly woman, silver-haired and slender, standing behind a modest microphone as though it were a stately pulpit. Her voice didn't just sing the gospel; it carried it. Each word rang out with both tenderness and power, weaving its way through the crowd like a thread binding us together.

I barely noticed the few curious glances turned my way. I wasn't there for them. I came drawn by the sound of that voice; the echo of something eternal stirring beneath her song.

The tent was hushed, reverent. Even the youngest children seemed still, as if mesmerized by a presence they didn't yet understand. And standing there among them, I felt it too, a shared hush, a sacred silence that wrapped around us like a warm wind before a storm. Then came the chorus, familiar, aching. A gospel refrain my mother used to sing when she thought no one was listening. *He touched me, oh, He touched me... and oh, the joy that floods my soul...*

The words hit hard. A lump rose in my throat, and the locks around my heart, rusted shut by years of pain, silence, and shame, began to rattle. Something deep inside me stirred, fragile and wild. The song, her voice, this moment, it all tugged at the gate I had sealed so long ago, threatening to undo me.

A sense of calm washed over me, and I closed my eyes and let the music carry me to a place of peace and serenity. A wave of pure relief washed over me from head to toe. Her beautiful rendition prepared my heart to hear the message of deliverance knocking at my heart's door. The preacher was powerful as he sermonized with conviction and authority. When he reached the climax of his message, he made a plea for salvation. His words echoed in my mind, "If Jesus Christ should come today or tomorrow, where would you be?"

Responding quietly to myself, I whispered, "I would bust hell wide open." Chuckling inwardly, a war raged within me. Should I admit the truth or continue hiding behind pretense or false piety? The battle between my heart and mind intensified as I grappled with the fear of judgment and the desire for authenticity. The weight of the question burdened my soul, overpowering the allure of maintaining appearances, foolish pride. With trembling hands and a lump in my throat, I contemplated breaking free from the shackles of pretense.

Taking a deep breath, I realized that acknowledging my vulnerability and confessing was the only way to find peace within myself. Taking courage, I made a solemn decision to let go of the mask and embrace the truth, however unsettling it may be. The battle for my soul hung in the balance. As if sensing my inner spiritual struggle, the pastor made his appeal once more. In response, I repeated the same words I had said earlier about 'hell.' The words, stark and raw, crossed my lips, plunging into my heart. Though I knew little of hell, the contrast with the slice of heaven I once experienced on earth was grim.

CHAPTER FOUR

Visiting church with my mom in the past held memories of peace, tranquility, and unmatched comfort. The hell I carried inside threatened to swallow me whole; black, heavy, relentless. I craved for even a moment of stillness; some place inside me that wasn't torn in half by grief, by shame, by the noise of everything I'd buried. My soul, bruised and fraying at the edges, cried out for rest. I dreamed of peace amidst the inner conflict screaming at full volume.

The darkness inside me surged, violent and relentless, as if every shadow I had ever tried to bury was now clawing its way to the surface. It felt like a battle in my chest, a storm of unseen forces staking claim to every unguarded corner of my mind. Fear. Shame. Rage. Despair. Each one whispering lies parading as truths, each one fighting to stay.

I clenched my fists at my sides, trembling, as if my body could barely contain what was happening inside. My thoughts were loud and wild, but somehow, I found my voice in chaos. Not a shout, but not a whisper either, just loud enough for my own ears to hear.

"God... whoever You are, wherever You are... I'm getting up. I'm walking toward the altar." The words came out broken, but they were real. Honest. They carried everything I had left. I lifted my face, heavy with emotion, and looked upward. Not because I expected to see anything, but because I needed Him to know I meant it. My voice cracked as I spoke again, this time softer, more fragile.

"If You're real... please. Don't let anyone touch me." I wasn't ready for hands on my shoulders or well-meaning strangers asking what was wrong. I couldn't explain it. I didn't want to. I just needed to move; I needed to make the walk from where I stood to wherever God might meet me. This wasn't about theatrics. It wasn't about appearances. It was about surrender.

I wasn't asking for a miracle; I was begging for mercy. One moment of untouched space. One moment when I could fall apart without interruption. One moment where God would hear me and come close.

I stood up, slowly and unsteadily, as if the very air around me had thickened. My legs felt like they belonged to someone else, numb, reluctant, but I forced them to move. The weight on my shoulders wasn't just emotional; it was physical, like I was carrying the accumulated sorrow of every moment I had stayed silent, every memory I had tried to outrun.

Step by step, I walked toward the altar. It wasn't a grand altar, just a simple space at the front of the tent, flanked by folding chairs and soft lights, but at that moment, it felt like sacred ground. I didn't come with elegant words or a rehearsed prayer. I came empty. I became desperate.

When I reached the front, I stopped. I closed my eyes. Holding my breath, unsure of what I expected, but not yet willing to leave. I didn't want anyone to lay a reassuring hand on me. I wasn't ready for that. Touch still felt dangerous, too close to wounds that hadn't healed. But still, I waited. Because beneath my fear of being touched was a deeper need: I didn't want to be invisible. I didn't want to suffer in silence anymore.

I wanted someone, *anyone,* to see me, not out of pity, but out of recognition. To look at me and somehow convey: *You're not crazy. You're not alone. You're not beyond help.*

I stood in the stillness, my heart exposed, tears threatening again. I waited not just for a sign from heaven, but for the simple mercy of being seen. As I stood, vulnerable and exposed, the congregation's hushed whispers echoed through the silent church. Yet, it offered a subtle comfort that I did not know I needed. With each passing moment, I felt the collective prayers and presence of the people around me.

Their prayers, soft, steady, and Spirit-filled, began to seep into places I had long kept sealed. Like water through cracks in stone, they gently chiseled the walls I had spent years building, dissolving layer by layer the defenses I once believed would keep me safe. But those defenses had only kept me trapped in silence, behind shame. And now my cheeks were wet; something was breaking.

The weight of my secret, the one I had guarded so well that I had almost convinced myself it wasn't real, had grown too heavy to carry. It pressed against my chest like a collapsed roof, and I felt myself suffocating under its weight. I had reached the edge of myself. The edge of my own capacity. The edge of silence. The edge of survival.

The darkness inside me clawed higher, threatening to swallow me whole. My grip on life, already loose, began to slip. My breath came in short, shallow bursts, and the pain I had tried to contain for so long finally surged to the surface. I couldn't hold it back any longer. Not the memories. Not the truth. Not the scream inside me begging to be set free. In that moment, I was ready.

Ready to say the words I had never said. Ready to rip the veil off the lie I had lived behind. I didn't care how many jaws would drop. I didn't care how much it might disrupt the polished image of our private, upscale community. The truth was more sacred than the illusion. And I was ready to unleash it. It was necessary.

But just as I stood trembling on the brink of that precipice, heart cracked wide open, soul raw with truth, a voice slithered into the silence. Sinister. Familiar.

It didn't shout. It whispered.

If you tell them, they'll never look at you the same again. You'll ruin everything. You'll destroy their image of her... and of you. They won't believe you anyway.

It was the voice of fear, cloaked in logic. The voice that had kept me quiet for years. The one that knew exactly which wounds to press to make me retreat. And for a moment, I hesitated, dangling between liberation and silence, between truth and self-preservation. My heart thundered. My fists were clenched. And I remain standing there, suspended in a holy war between what I had suffered and who I might become if I chose to speak.

The war inside me raged louder than the music, louder than the prayers around me. It was a brutal clash between confession and silence; between the freedom I desperately craved and the fear of unraveling everything I had ever tried to protect. My heart felt torn in two, on one side reaching for the light, the other shackled by the weight of consequences I couldn't fully name.

What would happen if I were to tell the truth? What would happen if the fragile image of strength I'd spent years building shattered under the weight of what I had to say? What would happen if people saw the broken, hurting, ashamed me? I was terrified. Terrified of being misunderstood. Terrified of being rejected. Terrified of the ripple effects, the fallout, the judgment. And yet, somewhere beneath that fear, in a place unmarked by shame, I knew *I couldn't carry it any longer.*

The silence was killing me. It had become a prison, a coffin for my soul. And though I wasn't ready to open my mouth to another human being, though the thought of speaking to someone face to face made my chest tighten with panic, I knew I had to start somewhere.

So, I turned inward. I steadied myself, trembling, but resolute and prepared to speak to the only One I dared trust with my whole truth, God. Gathering the pieces of my courage. I opened my mouth and began to pray, not with perfect words, but with the unfiltered, bleeding honesty of someone whose soul was bursting open.

Mindlessly, I continued talking, praying, and walking toward the front of the church. A few glanced my way, but their heads quickly bowed as they were engaged in their own personal struggles. No one touched me; I moved unopposed, in a trance-like state. The buzzing in my head subsided, giving way to the clear, distinct voice of the pastor. Each syllable pierced my soul, unhindered and profound. Standing on the edge of the spiritual realm, my mind, now a battlefield, was thrust into a fierce struggle for my soul.

I closed my eyes, surrendering to the invisible forces swirling around me. The weight of the decision I had to make pressed heavily on my chest as if the outcome of this inner struggle would determine the course of my life. With each passing second, I felt the enormity of the moment bearing down on me, questioning my very existence.

It was a choice between holding onto the trauma or embracing the unknown path that lay ahead. The weight of the decision seemed unbearable, but deep down I knew that I had to leap.

As I approached the altar, my heart raced, pounding so loudly I feared it might stop at any moment. Adrenaline surged through me, amplifying the inner turmoil. I struggled to catch my breath, summoning strength from the depths of my being. Dark whispers continued to cloud my thoughts, urging me to turn and flee, but I stood firm. I faced the foe, named fear, and told it to go to hell.

In that moment, I finally said it, not out loud, but deep within, where truth has no place to hide. I was exhausted, soul-deep weary. Tired of pretending. Tired of carrying weight. Tired of waking up every day with a smile that didn't reach my eyes and a silence that screamed inside me. I was sick and tired... of being sick and tired.

There was no more strength left to fake it. No more walls left to lean on. I had reached the end of the rope. And in that empty, hollow place, face to face with fear, doubt, and everything I'd been trying to outrun, I realized something had to change. I had nothing left to lose.

So, I looked upward, not with confidence, but with a shaky kind of desperation. I didn't have a polished prayer. I didn't have certainty. But I had a whisper of hope. And for the first time, maybe ever, I was ready to take a chance on Jesus.

CHAPTER FIVE

In an instant, a thought swept through me like a wind through an open door, and suddenly, I was no longer in the tent. The world around me shifted, and I found myself in a dim, suffocating room. The air was thick, the walls too close. The shadows clung to every surface, curling in the corners like they were alive. I knew this place. Not by its geography, but by the way it *felt*, like secrecy, like sin. A room not of this world, but of my soul.

He was there. The foe. Not in the flesh, but as a presence, cold, persuasive, watching. He sat across from me, eyes glinting with familiarity, lips curled in a smirk that knew all my secrets. And in that hidden, hell-lit place, we conspired, not with words shouted in anger, but with the quiet, deadly precision of pain sharpened into purpose.

We plotted.

We laid out a plan to expose Candace and make her answer for what she had done. I could feel the fire in my chest rise with every imagined scenario. I wanted justice. No! *I wanted revenge.* I wanted her to feel exposed, stripped bare before the world, the way she had left me stripped inside. I wanted her to hurt. *Make her pay,* the voice inside hissed. *She made you a prisoner. Drag her into the same chains. Ruin her.* And I wanted to.

Every fiber of my broken self-screamed for it. Not because it would make me whole, but because it was the only thing that made sense in the madness. But then, something shifted as if a cold wind blew out the fire. I felt my voice begin to falter. The words I'd formed in my mind lost their grit. My resolve trembled.

The rage was still there. Yes! But something else was rising beneath it. Grief. Loss. The terrible recognition of everything I had endured, everything that had been stolen. My mother's face, gentle, strong, gone, flashed through the darkness, and her absence hit me like a thunderclap. The pain of her death. The agony of her not being here to hold me, to protect me. The unwelcome transformation into becoming this broken version of her boy… it unraveled me. And with it came the memories, the *real* ones.

The mistreatment. The manipulation. The silence I had been forced to live inside. They rushed over me like a flood, drowning every ounce of vengeance with sorrow.

And just like that, the room began to blur. The walls fell away. The darkness peeled back. I was no longer a co-conspirator; I was just a boy. Wounded. Tired. Longing to be free. And then, I was back. Back in the tent, on the precipice of surrender. Heart pounding. Eyes open. Soul trembling.

"No!" I whispered through clenched teeth, shaking my head with what little strength I had left. I refused to let fear win, not this time. I was too tired, too hollowed out by months of pretending, carrying, breaking. Fear had been my master long enough. I didn't have the energy, or the will, to let it rule me anymore.

But surrender… surrender wasn't easy either.

Every step I tried to take felt like wading through quicksand; my legs heavy, my body resisting as if some invisible force was dragging me backward. I wasn't advancing. I was sinking. And it wasn't just my body; it was my soul. Inside, a storm raged. My

FROM BROKENNESS TO BEAUTY

spirit was torn at the seams.

The part of me that still clung to control, the part shaped by pain, silence, rage, fought against the invitation to let go. To trust. To open myself to Jesus, who I still wasn't sure would accept what He'd find inside me.

The pain in my chest tightened like a vice, crushing me from the inside out. My heart drummed wildly, as if trying to break free from its cage. A sharp pressure bloomed behind my eyes, and a dull ache crept up the back of my skull until my vision blurred. Stars danced in front of me, warning signs, flares of my body nearing collapse.

My knees buckled and I staggered. I should've stopped. I should've fallen. But something inside, something small, yet defiant, kept me moving. I didn't want to faint here, not on the cusp of a breakthrough, not at the threshold of freedom. So, I pushed. One trembling step. Then another. Forward in my body, forward in my spirit.

The harmonious voices of the choir filled the atmosphere, wrapping around my heart like a healing salve. Each note seemed to carry the backing of heaven, waging a silent war against the chaos that had long ruled my inner world. As the melody rose, something inside me began to break, gently, but undeniably. A wave of relief surged through my mind, and for the first time in what felt like an eternity, the pain began to retreat into the background.

In that sacred moment, the consuming thoughts of vengeance toward Candace dissolved. The darkness that once urged retaliation lost its grip. The hardened cuffs of resentment, which had latched onto my soul, fell off like chains finally broken. I exhaled the heaviness I didn't know I was still carrying. It was gone. And in its place, peace began to rise.

Shaking myself back to reality, I realized the hymn was still echoing through the sanctuary. Its words slice through my defenses like truth draped in melody. Each note seemed to call out the war inside me. My fists clenched instinctively, as if bracing for another wave of emotion I couldn't name. Then, almost without thought, my eyes lifted, drawn to the wooden cross standing quietly near the pulpit.

It wasn't just a symbol anymore. It was an anchor in the storm of my thoughts, a lifeline amid the flood of torment that had long ruled my mind. I felt as though I was sinking in quicksand. Each thought, each memory trying to drag me back into the prison of my pain. But as I locked eyes with that cross, something shifted. For the first time, I saw a future not framed by shame or vengeance, but by the hope of something... more.

Let go. Let go. Let go. A quiet command, not shouted, but steady. With trembling resolve, I unclenched the grip that hatred had on my heart. I let go of the handcuffs of rage, the silent craving for revenge, the fantasy of justice that would never bring peace. I released them, not because the pain had vanished, but because I could no longer afford to be ruled by it. It was a burden too heavy.

Under the soft glow of the moonlight filtering through stained glass, the wooden cross, simple and adorned by a red scarf, drew me in like a force beyond myself. My feet moved almost involuntarily; every step toward it dissolved darts of torment. And as I stood before it, vulnerable and undone, a revelation pierced through the wreckage inside me: **I needed Jesus.**

Not just to forgive. Not just to fix what was broken. I needed Him to carry the load I no longer could. I needed Him to save me from the version of myself molded by pain. That moment wasn't dramatic. Yet, it was powerful, life-changing, a rebirthing. It was Holy.

CHAPTER SIX

Approaching the altar with a sigh, the spirit of fear manifested before me, with a sinister grin stretching across his face. The dark beast looked hungrily at my soul. Holding a rope in his right hand engraved with my name, Charlie, and a seductively crafted bullhorn in his left.

Instantly, I felt something more than fear; I felt the pull of death and insanity squeezing my cranium. An indescribable sensation consumed me as I was supernaturally transported to hell, the place death had reserved for me. In this macabre realm, I was surrounded by the suffocating stench of sulfur and blood-curdling reverberations of screams.

Yet, even in the barren wasteland of my soul, where despair had laid claim and shadows had long taken root, a flicker, small but unrelenting, ignited within me. It was hope. Bruised, but alive. Fragile, yet fierce. And though darkness pressed in from every side, that ember refused to be snuffed out.

Something deeper, something sacred, stirred inside me; a holy boldness, rising like a tidal wave against everything that had tried to break me. With what little strength remained in my weary body, I threw myself at the altar. My breath ragged, my heart wide open, my soul bowed in desperation and reverence. I wasn't just kneeling; I was fully surrendering.

Then he came. Fear. That old tormentor. I felt his chilling presence draw near again. His clawed fingers, familiar and sinister, marked my forehead with the residue of shame. He sneered as he whispered lies, exhaling lust, seduction and entitlement into my face like a poisonous fog. He reminded me with mocking certainty: "You gave me permission. I still have rights here."

But before I could retreat into accustomed subordination, before I could bend to the echoes of old fetters, a more compelling voice thundered like a wave of power. Quiet, but commanding. Calm but filled with absolute authority: "Release him now, in Jesus' name." In an instant, the grin vanished from Fear's twisted face. His arrogance collapsed into horror. He recoiled, then slithered backward, stripped of his power, exposed by Glory. No words. No farewell. Just gone... and then sweet peace.

Real peace. Like warm, healing oil poured over open wounds. Like sunlight touching a soul long frozen. Ripples of it moved through me, settling into crevices where fear once ruled.

I lay there in awe, utterly unraveled. Not by fear, not by terror, but by the overwhelming authority of a voice I could not see. Crawling slowly to my knees, breath catching in my chest, I trembled under the cognizance of what had just taken place. The burden I had carried for so long, unspeakable, heavy, suffocating, had lifted. And in its place... serenity. Sacred. Holy.

I exhaled. It felt like the first time in years, and the air I released carried pain, shame, and darkness with it. In that stillness, I felt a descending presence, gentle but all-consuming. A divine embrace wrapped around me, not to crush me, but to hold every shattered piece of me together. Peace began to well up from within, quiet and pure, flowing through every hollow place in my soul. Tears slipped from my eyes, slow, steady, sacred. Not of sorrow, but of release. Of recognition. Of restoration.

Through the blur of my tears, I looked down. And there it

was, lying broken at the foot of the cross: the eros bullhorn. This twisted weapon was once used to shout lust, domination, and shame into my life. Now reduced to nothing but fine, powdered dust, stripped of its voice, shattered beyond repair.

Besides it, I saw the rope. The same ceremonial rope Candace had used to bind me. It was undone; every knot unraveled. No longer holding me. No longer naming me. And then I saw it. Where my name had once been engraved in torment, in accusation, a new name was written. Not mine, but His! JESUS CHRIST, etched in bold, red letters, marked the place of my deliverance. His name had replaced mine. His blood had bought and redeemed my story. In that moment, I knew I belonged to Him. He had set me free.

Jesus, the master shepherd, spoke, reassembling the fragments of my heart and renewing the adolescent boy within. He said, "I love you, and I knew you when you were in your mother's womb. Give me your life, and in my name, I will empower and robe you in spiritual authority to defeat fear and his demonic companions."

Overwhelmed, yet convinced I had made the right choice, I pivoted and resolved in my heart to follow the powerful voice. The same voice that reminded me in the graveyard that He was the Prince of Peace. My mother knew Him, and I wanted what she possessed. I took a deep breath and whispered, "I surrender."

Just then, the choir began to sing one of my mother's favorite songs, "The Potter Wants to Put You Back Together Again."[1]

---

[1] "The Potter Wants to Put You Back Together Again." (Traimine Hawkins)

The moment the melody filled the sanctuary, something inside me broke open. The lyrics didn't just echo in the room; they reverberated through my soul. That song became a sacred bridge between my pain and God's promise.

Each word formed a cast around the broken places in me, speaking life to what had long been dead. Mending me. I was no longer on bended knees; I was being transported. My body remained still, but my spirit journeyed to a place untouched by trauma, untouched by shame. An eternal place. A healing place.

My inner man began to rise, responding, reaching, receiving. I felt the words soaking through the walls I had built, washing over my mind, saturating the parched ground of my heart. I wasn't just hearing the song; I was becoming it. I was the broken vessel. I was the clay on the wheel. And the Potter, my Savior, was calling me back to the wheel, back to wholeness.

In that moment, I remembered the teapot. The one from Book Two[2], the story that mirrored so much of what I had buried, the cracks, the fire, the discarded pieces. That teapot had been shattered, just like me. Left dusty on a shelf. Forgotten. But then the Master Craftsman came. And instead of discarding it, He picked it up, embraced every fracture, and made it whole, not by erasing the cracks, but by redeeming them. Now, it was my turn.

Stepping into the room, Jesus, the Master Potter, took center

---

[2] Dr. Kayla Bullard Book #2 *"When Trauma Writes the Story Triumph Wins!"* A Story of Redemption and Renewal

stage. In my view, the church was transformed into a shop. A stone furnace burned brightly in the corner, wood chips littered the floor, and the smell of pine filled the air. Yielding to the supernatural moment, my body remained transfixed as my spirit succumbed to the promise, peace, and tranquility of the words of the song. "The Porter Wants to Put You Back Together Again" (Traimine Hawkins)

I was no longer just clay in the Potter's hands; I was the teapot being redeemed. A story of shame, now being poured out as a testimony of grace. The very places I thought disqualified me were being transformed into places of beauty and strength. I was finally ready to be made whole.

CHAPTER SEVEN

Healing my soul was the focus. With tender strength, Jesus Christ transported me into His workshop. A place alive with love, mercy, and the fire of transformation. In the shop, the Master Potter cradled me in love. And with precision, He pressed, shaped, and reformed what life experiences had shattered.

I was Charlie. His fractured, but chosen vessel of clay, spinning on the wheel of grace. Each turn refined me, each pressure point purged what no longer served His purpose. His breath hovered over me, His living water softened me, and His Word became the blueprint of my becoming. *'Yet you, Lord, are our Father. We are the clay; you are the potter; we are all the work of your hand.'* (Isaiah 64:8) In His hands, I wasn't discarded ; I was destined. Repaired, repurposed, and redefined for His glory

And just as the prophet described, I too was brought to the Potter's house. In the eyes of my spirit, I followed the Lord and beheld Him at work. There, I saw Him working at the wheel. His hands, steady. His gaze, unwavering. His movements, rhythmic with purpose at the wheel. He was forming a vessel from clay, but something within the pot was flawed. Still, He did not abandon it. Instead, with compassion in His gaze and mastery in His hands, He gently sprayed living water over the marred clay, softening its resistance.

Then, with tender deliberation, He broke the clay apart, piece by piece, not to destroy, but to prepare. Each fragment was placed into a basin already moistened with mercy, where it was remixed, reworked, and made pliable once again. When the texture was just right, yielded, surrendered, and ready, He began anew.

He pressed in closer. With holy intention, He began to reshape what was ruined. With unmatched precision and divine artistry, He shaped it into a new creation, more beautiful than before. No longer just a vessel, it became a sacred artifact, forged for glory. The Potter didn't rush or recoil; He redesigned me with care, crafting a new form that only He could envision. What once bore the evidence of misuse and shame now took on the contours of purpose and righteousness.

So, I went down to the potter's house, and I saw him working at the wheel. But the pot he was shaping from the clay was marred in his hands; so, the potter formed it into another pot, shaping it as seemed best to him. (Jeremiah 18:3 - 4) Both disorienting and breathtaking, it was a divine dismantling; a holy undoing of all that had once held me. I had surrendered my will, and the Potter took full authority, guiding me through the sacred process of becoming. His hands, skilled and sovereign, were not just shaping clay; they were redefining my very soul. My intellect, emotions, and will were being rewired under the magnificence of His glory.

Laid bare upon the altar, I was subdued, silent, and surrendered as Jesus worked undisturbed. Time stood still in that sacred space. I could feel Him probing gently, yet purposefully, molding the deep recesses of my heart and mind. His touch was tender, but it levied the tonnage of transformation. I was being made into something brand new, something I did not fully recognize, yet somehow it felt like home. Familiarity gave way to divine mystery, and in that mystery, I discovered comfort. I was not lost; I was being remade."

He touched every fiber of my being; nothing was overlooked. His healing was not partial; it was holy, complete, and consuming. With the precision of a divine Surgeon and the loving tenderness of a Father, the Master moved through the hidden corridors of my soul. He extracted the residue of trauma, the haunting images, the lingering sounds, the buried scents etched deep into my memory. Strand by strand, He unraveled what had entangled me.

As He worked intricately on my soul, my mind was becoming less clouded by confusion, my heart, less scarred by pain, and my will began to strengthen against fear. Then He whispered a truth more powerful than every lie I had ever believed: *"You are Mine."* In that moment, I wasn't just being healed, I was being claimed, restored, and reestablished as His beloved.

He was sculpting me into a version of myself I had never known. Now marked by grace, the Heavenly Father, my Redeemer, reached into the ambushed timeline of my life and restored what had been stolen. He took me back to the time and place when my innocence was taken, not to reopen the wound, but to redeem it.

There, in that vulnerable place of pain, He washed me with His blood. He removed the heaviness of shame, the sting of guilt, and the ache of sorrow. His presence rewrote the memories with redeeming love. He gave me a recompense for the time that was stolen. And then for a second time came the whisper, gentle, holy, unmistakable: *'You are forgiven.'* That whisper was more than words   ; it was healing. It was music to my soul; it was the sound of freedom being sung over me.

Next, I was transported to the foot of the Cross, where my redemption was sealed in blood. The blood of Jesus flowed, cleaning and healing me everywhere there was pain, marking the beginning of my bodily restoration. The wounds I had inflicted upon myself, born out of despair and silence dissolved. The scars left by the sexual ropes of bondage vanished. The rope burns on my wrist that once represented abuse and trauma were supernaturally and physically erased.

Then came the stillness. The tormenting ring in my ears, the aftermath of the lab explosion, ceased in an instant. The loud voice of rejection, abandonment, and guilt that haunted me day and night was hushed by the sovereign voice of Truth. One by one, the lies were uprooted and, in their place, the Word, his words, were planted. He didn't just heal me, He rewrote the narrative etched into my body, mind, soul, and spirit with love, peace, mercy, and power.

The simple yet sacred words, *"I surrender"*, became the key that unlocked a deeper dimension of divine submission. In that holy space, I yielded   entirely to the hands of the Craftsman. Wrapped in the comfort of His peace, I let go, exhaling a long, trembling breath as the load I had carried lifted from my soul. The suffocating darkness that had once cloaked me dissipated in the light of His presence.

With my surrender, the work of healing surged forward. Wholeness began to take root. The walls I had built to protect my heart, walls built in fear and disappointment, crumbled in the presence of perfect love. Restoration flowed in like warm oil, saturating every dry and weary place within me. What once imprisoned me began to break apart, replaced by a stirring I hadn't known before, the gentle, holy desire to live... to breathe... to begin again.

The pastor's words rang out with billowing authority, resounding through the deepest chambers of my soul: *"The Potter wants to put you back together again."* That declaration pierced through every layer of shame. He, Jesus, knew everything, every fracture, every failure, and yet   His love remained. Unrelenting. Restorative. Ready.

We all need a Savior. And Jesus, in His mercy, desires that none should perish, but that all would come to repentance. With nothing left to prove, I   lay prostrate on the floor, no pretense, no resistance, just a surrendered vessel before the Cross. I turned my gaze upward, eyes flowing with tears, and whispered, *"Thank You."*

With slow, reverent movement, I adjusted my posture and bowed my head in humility. As the prayers of those around me rose like incense, I added my voice to theirs, trembling, but sincere. Each word of the prayer was like a careful stitch, sewing up the ripped fabric of my soul. Healing me, mending me, with every whispered truth, every act of surrender, every breath and confession drawn in faith.

"Lord, I confess I'm a sinner in need of a Savior.

Forgive every sin I have committed.

Wash me with your blood. I believe that you died for me.

Come into my life and make me whole.

In Jesus' name. Amen!"

As the final words left my lips, a wave of unspeakable joy washed over me, from head to toe. Fresh tears streamed down my face, but these were not tears of pain. They were a roar from the soul, shouting freedom. I remained at the altar no longer haunted, no longer crushed. Fear had lost its evil grip. The pressure shattered. Suicide silenced. The foe that once hunted me was now beneath my feet.

Relief surged through me like a mighty river, washing away years of sorrow in a single tide. This unspeakable joy, uncontainable, pure and holy, burst forth in laughter that felt like healing in motion. With no hesitation, I unfolded myself, stretching out prostrate on the floor, overwhelmed with gratitude too deep for words. I rolled across the sanctuary floor, uncaring of who watched, because at that moment, I knew I was free. Free. Redeemed. Made new. A heavenly, Jesus-conducted jailbreak had occurred, and I was no longer the same. Free.

In the surge of freedom I had never known, I rolled without hesitation, free in my body, clear in my mind, and alive in my spirit. The chains that had once bound me in shame, fear, and silence had been broken by the power of freedom in Christ. I was released from the mental yokes that held me captive, released from the trauma of Candice's cruel manipulation… released from the lingering grief of my mother's death.

I was released from the agony of rape and the deep wounds of exploitation. Released from the crushing magnitude of hidden secrets, I dared not speak. Released from the torment of unforgiveness that had gripped my heart like a vice. In that precious moment, I was no longer surviving; I was free and alive. And freedom was exhilarating. I had been marred, shattered, and sunken in the mire, but in the hands of the Master Potter, Jesus reshaped me. He restored the broken and breathed new life into what I thought was beyond repair.

As I rose from the ground, joy continued to surge through me, raw, real, and undeniable. Yet, even in the midst of that sacred celebration, a wave of unexpected loneliness swept over me. I paused, searching inwardly. There, in the quiet depths of my soul, I sensed an empty space, a place that had once been gripped by darkness, now cleansed and hollow. But it wasn't emptiness I felt. It was an invitation. That space was no longer a void, it was being sanctified, prepared to become a dwelling place for the Holy Spirit. As the Scripture declares, "Do you not know that your body is the temple of the Holy Spirit?" (1 Corinthians 6:19). God was not just delivering me; He was making His home within me.

The familiar strangers, fear, depression, and the other dark spirits that once ruled my heart now lingered at a distance, watching in gloom. Their absence felt unsettling, like the sudden quiet after a long, chaotic storm. Out of habit, I called for fear to return. He crept forward, responding like a loyal friend, but something unseen, yet undeniably powerful, stopped him in his tracks. He tried again, inching closer. Still, the barrier held firm, holy, unshakable, and alive. The space he once occupied now belonged to Someone greater.

I was no longer his dwelling. Fear no longer had legal access. Shame had been evicted. Darkness had met a closed door. The rooms of my soul that had once been residence to spirits of torment were now filled with the light of truth. I had become the temple of the Holy Spirit. I was now sacred, set apart, and sealed. His presence didn't just visit me; it inhabited me. He filled the conflicted places with peace, the weak places with power, and the barren places with purpose. I was no longer a vessel of pain; I was a sanctuary of glory. What once was a battleground had become holy ground.

One by one, each dark spirit retreated: abuse, anger, bitterness, burden, confusion, depression, despair, destruction, disgust, distrust, doubt, dread, frustration, grief, guilt, hatred, hopelessness, insecurity, loneliness, murder, nervousness, pain, passivity, pity, rejection, resentment, restlessness, retaliation, shame, tension, unforgiveness, unworthiness, violence, and worry each slipping away into the shadows from whence they came.

Trauma shaped my identity, and fear dictated my every move. And without notice, rejection had cunningly slipped in and made himself at home. Together, the entire cohort had driven, directed, and governed my thoughts. I had been manipulated by the master of lies called Deceit. The constant ache in my soul was the open door, the gateway that welcomed the floodgates of demonic oppression and depression. Their presence consumed my youth, muting my voice and distorting my purpose. Even further, trauma had influenced my identity; fear controlled my actions, and rejection secured my pain.

Ignorantly, I had opened the door of my heart and given these spirits access. Ushered in by loss, abuse, and trauma, these demonic influences shaped my choices and controlled my life. But now, standing in the aftermath, no longer bound or ensnared by their traps, I basked in the light of new freedom. My displaced companion, *"Fear,"* no longer ruled me. I was free, truly free.

In the middle of my unhinging, Jesus stepped in. He didn't knock; He came with authority. He silenced every lie. With one touch, He loosened every chain. His light broke through, exposing the roots of deception and replacing them with my real identity, healing, and peace. I had broken free from the suffocating chokehold of sin, and for the first time, I could breathe. Where sadness once ruled, an unexpected peace rushed in, followed by a joy so pure, it caught me by surprise. As the awareness of what had just taken place settled over me, I felt it deeply: my sincere acceptance of Jesus as Savior.

My *yes*, had shattered every chain and opened the floodgates of heaven. Now the Holy Spirit is the sole occupant of the chambers of my heart.

Tears poured from a place words could never touch, deep, raw, and unrestrained. They came not from the surface, but from the hidden corridors of my heart, long sealed by pain and silence. Each drop carried away years of sorrow, disappointment, and buried grief. And with every release came a wave of healing, not just emotional, but spiritual. That moment of unfiltered weeping became my offering, my surrender. In those tears, I wasn't breaking down; I was breaking free.

A sweet and steady peace wrapped itself around my soul, quieting the inner chaos left behind by Candice's torment. What once felt like a war zone within me was now still. Jesus had not only saved me, but He had also made me whole. Choosing to forgive became the key that unlocked another facet of my freedom.

Forgiveness untied the ropes of resentment and pain that had stealthily oppressed me. But the true breakthrough came when, led by the gentle prompting of the Holy Spirit, I found the courage to forgive myself. That moment was not just freeing, it was revolutionary. And I finally stood in the light, no longer bound by who I had been, but awakened to who I was becoming, who I was meant to be. As I extended grace inwardly, another heavy blanket of emotional and spiritual weight fell loose. I felt it, like shackles falling from my soul, one by one. A sacred unburdening was taking place, and freedom was no longer a distant hope; it was happening within me.

I was no longer housing fear, but the indwelling presence of the **Holy Spirit**. The territory once ruled by anxiety, shame, torment, and the like, had been reclaimed by the power of God. The wounds of the past were gone; they no longer had the power to define or confine me. Fear, which once sat on the throne of my thoughts, whispering lies and reigning over my identity, had been dethroned. His governance, once constant and oppressive, had been ousted.

Where panic once resided, peace now reigns. Where condemnation screamed, grace now speaks. Where darkness loomed, light now shines without apology.

The Holy Spirit, my Comforter, Counselor, and Defender, has taken residence in the deepest chambers of my soul. I was filled, led, and secured by the Spirit of the Living God. Fear no longer has a hold on me because Perfect Love has moved in (1 John 4:18). I am not the same person as I was when I walked into that sanctuary bound and broken. Because where the Spirit of the Lord is, there is freedom (2 Corinthians 3:17). And I am living proof.

What once anchored my body, mind, and spirit in cycles of shame and sorrow was now replaced by radiant clarity. Peace, deep and undisturbed, settled into the empty spaces. *I was no longer conquered by neglect and abuse; I was free!*

CHAPTER EIGHT

When Charlie rose from that floor, I, guilt, was left behind. For so long, I had wrapped myself around his soul like a second skin. I whispered shame into his thoughts, replayed his failures on repeat, and kept him chained to what he had done, what he had endured, and what he believed he could never overcome. I made him believe that he wasn't worthy of forgiveness, that his past was too stained to be redeemed.

And for a long time, he believed me.

But then… something shifted. Charlie called on the name of Jesus. He didn't just speak it; he surrendered to it. And at that moment, everything changed. The truth of scripture came alive: *"Therefore, if anyone is in Christ, he is a new creation. The old has passed away; behold, all things have become new."* (2 Corinthians 5:17).

I, guilt, had no defense against that kind of love. No weapon in my arsenal could stand against the power of true repentance and divine forgiveness. I tried to cling to him as he stood, but I couldn't. The dominance I once had over him lifted, and I was silenced.

You see, guilt isn't just a feeling   ; it's a prison. It distorts identity, delays healing, and disconnects the soul from hope. Left unchecked, guilt festers into shame, self-condemnation, and cycles of self-destruction. But when brought to the cross, guilt loses its stronghold.

Charlie's past wasn't erased; it was redeemed. And that's the power of grace. In Christ, guilt is no longer the final word. Freedom is. Forgiveness is. Wholeness is. When Charlie got up, I stayed behind, buried beneath mercy, silenced by love, and dismantled in the light of truth.

When Charlie got up from that floor, it wasn't just a physical act   ; it was a resurrection moment. It mirrored what Jesus Christ did on Calvary. After bearing the full weight of sin, shame, and guilt on the cross, Jesus didn't stay buried. On the third day, He rose, triumphant, glorified, and forever victorious over death, sin, and the grave.

In the same way, Charlie didn't just rise   ; he rose *from something.* He got up from guilt, from shame, from everything that once buried him emotionally, spiritually, and mentally. That floor became his personal Calvary, his place of surrender, death to the old and the beginning of new life.

The power of the cross isn't just that Jesus died   ; it's that He *got up.* And when He rose, He proved that nothing, not sin, not death, not guilt, could hold Him. That same resurrection power met Charlie on the floor that day. It lifted him, not just to his feet, but to a new identity, a new authority, a new beginning.

As the Scripture says in 2 Corinthians 5:17, *"Therefore, if anyone is in Christ, he is a new creation. The old has passed away; behold, all things have become new."* Charlie stood not as the adolescent he was, but as the young man God always intended him to be.

And just as the tomb couldn't keep Jesus, shame and guilt couldn't keep Charlie. When Jesus got up, He carried victory in His hands. When Charlie got up, he carried freedom in his soul. One was the Savior of the world. The other: A living testimony of that Savior's love.

To the one still lying on the floor, buried under the curse of guilt, regret, and self-condemnation, this is your call to arise. You don't have to stay there. Just as Charlie stood up from that sacred place of surrender, so can you. *The same resurrection power*

***that lifted Jesus from the grave and lifted Charlie from the
ground is available to lift you, right now.***

You are not beyond redemption. You are not disqualified.
You are not too broken or too far gone. The voice of guilt may
try to keep you silent, but the voice of God is more powerful,
and He's calling you by name.

*"There is therefore now no condemnation for those who are in Christ
Jesus."* (Romans 8:1)

"If the Son sets you free, you will be free indeed." (John 8:36)

"He has removed our sins as far from us as the East is from the West."
(Psalm 103:12)

"Come now, let us reason together," says the Lord. *"Though your sins
are like scarlet, they shall be as white as snow."* (Isaiah 1:18)

Jesus didn't die so you could live in shame. He died and rose,
so you could live in **freedom**. The Cross is enough. His blood is
enough. His love is more than enough.

So, rise. Not in your strength, but in His. Rise and leave guilt
at the feet of Jesus. Rise and walk in the newness of life. Rise and
become who you were always created to be.

Because in Christ, you are forgiven. You are free. And you are
deeply, eternally loved.

CHAPTER NINE

In a world that frantically races forward and rarely stops to feel or process, the pain of men who have endured sexual abuse is not just overlooked, it is buried. Buried beneath society's indifference. Dismissed as a weakness. Ignored out of discomfort. Denied because it doesn't fit the narrative.

Sidestepped because of misconceptions about what men and boys should be able to withstand. Their suffering hides behind forced smiles, silent stares, and the heavy armor society demands they wear. They're told to "man up," to be strong, to stay silent, because vulnerability, for a man, is falsely perceived as weakness.

So, they lock it away. The shame. The confusion. The rage. They bury it deep, beneath layers of cultural pressure and personal torment. The silence they carry is not resilience; it's a mask, carefully worn to conceal the torment within. But silence doesn't heal. It haunts. And behind that quiet facade, the pain doesn't fade... it deepens.

Beneath the bandage of silence lies a wound that screams, an ache that pulses endlessly, a hidden fracture tearing at the core of identity. This isn't just pain; it's a cry for recognition. Yet, until their suffering is acknowledged, until their voices are no longer silenced by fear or shame, true healing will remain just out of reach.

These men are not weak. They are survivors, warriors bearing invisible scars from a war they were never prepared to fight. Their strength is forged in isolation, in silence, in agony. And we must ask ourselves: what does it say about us, about our compassion, our humanity, when we choose to look away from the brokenness of those who were never given the safety to speak?

Consider Charlie, just a teenage boy yet carrying a weight no child should ever be asked to bear. His innocence was violated in the shadows; stolen by hands that should have protected him. And in the silence that followed, Charlie didn't just lose his voice, he lost a part of himself. He walked through life cloaked in shame, gripped by confusion he couldn't explain, and shackled by a lie that told him he was weak because of what had been done to him.

He feared the world's response, the judgment in their eyes, the questions he couldn't answer, the labels he might never escape. So, he said nothing. Not because he didn't want to speak, but because silence felt safer than disbelief and ridicule.

Charlie could be anyone. He could be your brother. Your son. Your nephew. Your best friend. He could be your father, sitting across the table, laughing at your jokes, showing up for work, going through the motions. Functioning on the outside while quietly unraveling within.

This is the reality too many men live with: suffering in silence because no one ever made it safe for them to speak. And unless we dare to look beyond the surface, we'll keep missing the pain that hides behind their show of strength, and the healing that's waiting to begin if only someone would truly see them.

Charlie experienced severe and long-lasting effects from the trauma he went through. [3]According to renowned trauma expert Dr. Bessel van der Kolk, when emotional or psychological

---

[3] The Body Keeps the Score: Brain, Mind, and Body in the Healing of Trauma, Dr. Bessel Van Der Kolk, 2014

wounds go untreated, they can distort a victim's sense of reality and disrupt the body's natural ability to function. People may turn to substances like drugs or alcohol in a desperate attempt to dull the pain, to silence the noise within.

These temporary escapes may offer a brief sense of relief, a momentary numbness from the unbearable weight of what the mind cannot forget. But trauma doesn't vanish with intoxication. The brain, especially one impacted by trauma, continues to replay the past like a broken record, uninvited, unresolved, and relentless.

According to trauma experts like Dr. Bessel van der Kolk, traumatic experiences become imprinted in the body and the brain, disrupting the nervous system, impairing memory processing, and altering emotional regulation. Even long after the event has passed, the body responds as if the danger is still present, keeping the person locked in a state of hypervigilance, anxiety, or emotional numbness.

When healthy coping mechanisms are unavailable or inaccessible, many survivors reach for anything that offers a sense of control or relief, even if it slowly destroys them. But numbing pain is not the same as healing it, and true healing begins when the trauma is acknowledged, confronted, and safely processed in the presence of compassion and truth (2014, p. 44).

Unlike physical wounds, the trauma of sexual abuse doesn't always leave visible scars. It often disguises itself in anger, depression, addiction, emotional detachment, anxiety, or cycles of self-destruction. Many men, like Charlie, struggle with their sense of identity, masculinity, and worth. They question their value. Some even question their faith or wonder if healing is truly possible.

What makes male sexual abuse especially devastating is not only the trauma itself, but the suffocating silence that surrounds it. In our culture, there is little room for men to process their pain and even less space for them to voice it.

From an early age, many boys are conditioned to suppress vulnerability. They're told to "man up," to toughen up, to bury their emotions, to walk it off, to take it like a man. When abuse occurs, this conditioning becomes a prison. Some are led to believe that sexual abuse only happens to weak men, or worse, that real men shouldn't be affected by it at all. The result is a soul-deep isolation, where shame festers and healing feels out of reach.

Dr. Bessel van der Kolk explains that trauma is not just an event that happens; it's the imprint it leaves on the body and the brain. He writes that "traumatized people chronically feel unsafe inside their bodies," and when that trauma is silenced, especially in men who are told not to feel or speak, it often manifests as anxiety, depression, addiction, or even physical illness. The brain's alarm system, particularly the amygdala, becomes hyperactive, making it difficult to distinguish past threats from present safety. And without safe spaces for expression and integration, many men live in a state of constant internal warfare.

Abuse has no gender bias. Pain doesn't discriminate. And yet, society still struggles to validate the suffering of men who have been violated. Until we dismantle the false narratives that equate masculinity with emotional suppression, countless men will remain hidden in the shadows of their trauma, unheard, unseen, and unhealed.

Elie Wiesel, Holocaust survivor, author, and Nobel Peace Prize laureate, once spoke a truth that still reverberates in the hearts of those carrying unseen wounds. In his 1986 acceptance speech, he said, *"Trauma does not discriminate, and silence only deepens the wound."* These words reach into the quiet corners where pain is often hidden, and they speak directly to the men whose trauma has been buried beneath layers of cultural expectation, stigma, and fear.

For so many men, suffering becomes a private war, fought behind stoic faces, beneath the weight of messages that tell them to stay strong, stay silent, and never show weakness. But Wiesel's words remind us that trauma knows no boundaries. It crosses gender, age, and background. It reaches deep into the soul, into the sacred places no one else can see, places where pain flourishes in isolation and where silence becomes a second form of violence.

The trauma men experience is real. It is raw. And it is often left unspoken, not because it lacks depth, but because the world hasn't yet made space for their truth. But Wiesel's legacy urges us to listen, to break the silence, and to remember that healing begins not only with acknowledgment, but with compassion.

Wiesel reminded the world of a sobering truth: silence does not protect the wounded; it isolates them. It locks pain behind walls no one can see, where it festers in darkness and shame. When our voices are silenced by fear, by stigma, or by the belief that no one will understand, the trauma only digs deeper.

But healing begins when the silence is shattered, when pain is given language. When truth is spoken aloud and met, not with judgment, but with compassion, it takes courage to confront what hurts the most, to face the memories, to name the wound, to reach for healing. But that courage opens the door to freedom. When we begin to listen, to believe, and to hold space for their stories, we open the door for transformation, not just for individual men, but for a more compassionate and honest world.

In honoring Wiesel's words, we affirm a powerful truth: every story matters. Every wound is worthy of light. And no matter how deep the pain runs, no life is beyond the reach of redemption. Speaking our truth is not weakness; it is strength. And it is the first step toward reclaiming the wholeness we were always meant to walk in.

In a world that often portrays men through a distorted lens of dominance, invincibility, and emotional suppression, it can be incredibly difficult for men to step forward and admit they've been victims of sexual abuse, especially when the perpetrator is a woman. Yet the Bible paints a different picture of manhood. It shows us that men are not just warriors and leaders, they are also sons, servants, shepherds, and stewards of God's heart. They are created in the image of God (Genesis 1:27), with emotions, dignity, and the capacity to feel deeply.

Societal expectations often leave little room for men to grieve, to be vulnerable, or to seek healing, but Scripture does not silence the brokenhearted; it draws them close. Psalm 34:18 declares, *"The Lord is close to the brokenhearted and saves those who are crushed in spirit."* That promise is not limited by gender. God does not dismiss the pain of His sons.

When a man is wounded, especially by something as violating as abuse, his pain is not a mark of weakness; it is a cry for restoration. And the God of Scripture is a restorer. He is the One who binds up wounds (Psalm 147:3), who gives beauty for ashes (Isaiah 61:3), and who redeems what was stolen. True manhood is not defined by silence or stoicism; it is defined by truth, humility, and the willingness to step into the light of God's healing.

If men cannot find help or support in a world that imposes specific sexual expectations on them, how can they seek genuine assistance in a society that dictates their behavior towards the opposite sex? This dilemma presents an opportunity for the church to take a stand and proclaim that they have the answer. Through Jesus Christ, the church is empowered to set captives free. The church can offer men a spiritual solution to alleviate their pain from sexual abuse.

Generally, followers of Christ share the belief that unresolved trauma will dominate and corrupt a person entirely. When trauma is left unaddressed, it doesn't simply fade ; it festers. Neglected trauma can manifest as mental illness, physical symptoms, spiritual unrest, and in some cases, even death. Medical researchers have consistently shown that untreated trauma increases the risk of self-harm, substance abuse, and suicidal behavior. Without intervention, what starts as an invisible wound can evolve into a life-altering crisis, one that not only consumes the individual but also ripples outward, affecting families, relationships, and entire communities (Dr. Bessel van der Kolk, *The Body Keeps the Score*, 2014).

Untreated trauma not only affects the mind and body, but it can also leave individuals spiritually exposed. In some cases, unresolved wounds can open doors to supernatural oppression, including the influence of demonic entities. For a deeper exploration of this reality, see [4]Book #1, ***Help, I Need***

---

[4] Dr Kayla Bullard, Book #1 When Trauma Writes the Story: Triumph Wins! *Help! I Need Therapy. No! I Need Deliverance.*

Therapy, No, I Need Deliverance, which examines the connection between trauma, demons, and the need for spiritual deliverance. How a person's body responds to trauma and how the mind engages in healing significantly impacts their ability to receive both medical and spiritual intervention. True restoration requires addressing the whole person, spirit, soul, and body.

Seeking professional help is a vital step in confronting trauma and breaking the cycle of its damaging effects. I firmly believe that true healing is most effective when medical intervention and spiritual care work together in harmony. God, the ultimate Healer, has equipped professionals with the wisdom and tools to treat the mind and body, and through His Word and Spirit, He restores the soul.

Yet countless men continue to suffer in silence, not because they are unwilling to heal, but because they lack a safe space to seek help without fear of judgment, shame, or ridicule. For healing to begin, we must create an environment where vulnerability is not seen as weakness, but as strength, where faith and therapy walk hand in hand, and where every man knows he is seen, supported, and worthy of restoration.

In the church, it is important to create safe spaces for men to share their stories and heal. By doing so, we can work towards dismantling the stigma surrounding male victims of sexual abuse and paving the way for a more compassionate and healthy society.

Charlie displayed signs of mental instability and self-harm, indicative of his unhealthy state of mind. His apparent enjoyment of explosive distractions hinted at an impending breakdown. Bound by shame and confusion, he struggled with guilt over his predicament, which hindered him from seeking attention. His mind became a battleground, torn between the desire for sex, help, and the fear of judgment, which kept him trapped in his own torment. The weight of his emotions grew heavier with each passing day and threatened him to make grave decisions for his well-being and mental stability.

The Church must wake up; we are losing our men by the thousands. While the world grows louder with hypersexualized messages and distorted views of masculinity, many men are suffering in silence. The overstimulation and sensationalism of sex in our culture have made it increasingly difficult for men to report sexual abuse or misconduct. They fear being perceived as weak, emasculated, or less than what society expects of them.

This fear is compounded by a dangerous misconception: that real men must always be dominant, fierce like tigers, unshaken, self-sufficient. But that image leaves no room for brokenness, no space for vulnerability, no pathway to healing. It clashes violently with the reality that even strong men need support, care, and community. As a result, many choose silence over shame, isolation over misunderstanding, and pride over the risk of being seen as fragile.

The Church must be a place where men can lay down the false expectations of the world and be embraced by the truth of God's Word, that strength is not the absence of struggle, but the courage to seek healing. Until we create environments where men are free to speak, to weep, to confess, and to be restored, we will continue to lose them not just from our pews, but from their God-given purpose.

This societal expectation of dominance creates barriers for men when it comes to acknowledging and addressing their own vulnerabilities. This internal conflict can lead to profound consequences for a man's mental and emotional well-being, often resulting in isolation and a reluctance to seek help.

Without addressing these societal expectations, many men will continue to suffer in silence, enduring unnecessary hardships. By acknowledging the pain of men through providing sound spiritual support, we can assist in creating an environment where men feel safe to seek the help they need. It is time to break down the barriers and empower boys and men to speak out and heal from the traumas they have experienced.

A spiritual approach necessitates empathy and understanding, as well as a dedicated effort to challenge societal norms and foster a culture of Christ-centered support and compassion for male survivors of sexual abuse. It is imperative to advocate for spiritual resources and services tailored to the unique needs of male survivors. But Charlie's story doesn't end in silence. Like men who have suffered the same, the message remains the same; that manhood is not defined by the absence of pain, but by the willingness to face it and overcome it. To every man still living in silence: you are not alone.

You are not less of a man because of what was done to you.

You are not disqualified from healing, love, or purpose.

Your story matters.

Your voice matters.

And your healing is possible.

There is a safe place in the arms of Jesus, a Redeemer who binds up the brokenhearted and restores what was lost. There is no shame in your healing, only strength in your survival and glory in your restoration.

"He heals the broken-hearted and binds up their wounds." (Psalm 147:3)

"The Lord is close to the brokenhearted and saves those who are crushed in spirit." (Psalm 34:18)

"For I know the plans I have for you," declares the Lord, "plans to prosper you and not to harm you, plans to give you a future and a hope." (Jeremiah 29:11)

Men, it's time to break the silence and to tell the truth.

To let go of shame.

And to begin again!

CHAPTER TEN

The Bible is filled with accounts of individuals who received divine help in the face of overwhelming life struggles. These situations not only controlled their present, but left lasting marks that could easily be recognized as traumatic. These encounters weren't just emotional; they were deeply spiritual and often led to catastrophic consequences without divine intervention.

Take David, for example. He was a man after God's own heart, yet still a man prone to choices, some wise, others devastating. Like many today, David made a decision that spiraled into a consequence he was unprepared to carry. What he wrestled with wasn't just guilt or regret; it was a soul-deep wound that no human effort could heal.

His inner turmoil required more than time or counsel; it demanded divine intervention. Only God could reach into the depths of David's heart and provide the spiritual healing and restoration he desperately needed. His story reminds us that no matter how tangled the mess we create, the mercy and power of Jesus Christ remain strong enough to deliver us, even from the burdens we bring upon ourselves. So, imagine the sufficiency of grace for messes that have been thrust upon us.

King David's candid story begins in 2 Samuel chapter 11. Instead of going to war, the King decided to stay home. The details of why he stays home are unknown; however, during his sabbatical, he saw a woman taking a bath. He inquired about her and found out she was Bathsheba, the wife of Uriah the Hittite, who was away at war. The woman Bathsheba interested him, and he demanded her attention.

Consumed by lust, knowing that she was married, King David committed adultery. He impregnates Bathsheba and devises a plan to cover his steps. To conceal his actions, King David summons Bathsheba's husband, Uriah, from the battlefield, hoping that he will sleep with her and believe the child to be his own. Uriah, however, chooses not to enjoy any of the comforts of home while his comrades are still on the battlefield. His unwavering loyalty becomes a thorn in King David's side, leading to even more tragic outcomes.

David contrives a plan to murder her husband. This scandal would lead to a tragic sequence of events, with far-reaching consequences for the entire kingdom. Bathsheba marries the King after mourning the death of her husband. Despite his powerful position, David's actions would have a profound impact on the future of his reign and the lives of those around him.

The Lord was displeased, and he sent the prophet Nathan to address the King. Using an allegory, the prophet tells the King a story that deeply angers him. In his anger, David condemns the antagonist in the story and demands his death. The prophet then confronts David, revealing that he is the man spoken about in the allegory. Nathan stood before King David, his eyes filled with conviction, and delivered a message from the Lord: "O King, hear the words of the Almighty. You have sinned greatly against Him, and the consequences shall be severe." Because of his sin, the child born from his affair with Bathsheba would die.

Overwhelmed with guilt and remorse, David humbly confesses his sin to the Lord.

Details of David's emotional state were skillfully penned in Psalm 51, a widely recognized Psalm of forgiveness. In this powerful Psalm, King David appeals to God for mercy and forgiveness after his transgressions with Bathsheba. He expresses deep remorse and asks for a clean heart and a renewed spirit. David's heartfelt plea for forgiveness and cleansing echoed the depths of his sorrow and his desperate desire to be reconciled with God.

Through David's honest and humble confession, he seeks not only forgiveness but also a complete transformation of his inner being. This Psalm exposes the depth of the King's heart and the anguish he endured due to his deliberate actions. David pours out his heart, acknowledging his wrongdoing and crying out to the Lord for spiritual help. His pleas, "have mercy, blot out, wash me, cleanse me", express a desperate cry for forgiveness and purification. His words reveal the pure honesty and vulnerability of his soul as he seeks reconciliation with the Lord.

Through his prayers, David exemplifies the humility and repentance essential for seeking God's grace and mercy. David wrestles with mental anguish as memories of his sin torment him. In Psalm 51:3-4, he declares, "My sin is ever before me," vividly portraying the state of his mind. He is haunted by constant memories of his transgression. His honest admission of his mistakes and genuine remorse demonstrate the humility and repentance needed to ask for God's grace and mercy. It serves as a powerful testimony of his desire to change and grow spiritually.

The Bible teaches that healing is available to any individual who confesses Jesus Christ as Lord and Savior. Jesus is a healer, and he died so that believers could experience and be recipients of physical and spiritual healing in their own lives. He wants his followers to live in healing and good health. This concept is central to the Christian faith and the belief in the power of healing through spiritual reconciliation.

David's use of words like "my transgressions, my iniquity, my sin" emphasizes his accountability for his actions. Spiritual healing is portrayed as a crucial path to freedom, and King David earnestly sought help from Jehovah God to heal his shame and repent of his sinful deeds. In his heartfelt prayers, David acknowledged his flaws and sought forgiveness for the pain he had caused, yearning for a renewed spirit that would guide him back towards righteousness.

As he confessed his transgressions, David humbled himself before God, knowing that only through divine intervention could he find redemption and solace for his troubled soul.

Man is a three-part being, spirit, soul, and body (II Thessalonians 5:23). The profound depths of David's sins and regrets necessitated significant healing in every aspect of his life. His spirit needed restoration, his soul needed healing, and his body needed strength to carry on.

King David's issues surpassed natural and humanistic solutions. His expressive soul-searching lament in Psalm 51 bordered on torture. He experienced trauma because of a sexual decision that he made, compounded by lies, deception, and murder. His pain delves into the realm of the supernatural, leaving David feeling increasingly isolated and hopeless.

Counseling was not enough. David required supernatural intervention before he would ever be able to confront the damage he had inflicted upon himself, his wife, his children, and the nation of Israel.

The king needed spiritual healing himself to remove the contamination of sin from his body, soul, and spirit. Acknowledging his shame and need for help, he cried out,

"Create in me a clean heart, O God, and renew a right spirit within me." "Cast me not away from your presence, and take not your Holy Spirit from me," he prayed with desperation, seeking redemption and restoration.

Turning to the source of true freedom, he found hope in the promise of healing and forgiveness. With tears streaming down his face, he clung to these timeless words, knowing that only through divine intervention could he find solace for his tormented soul. With each word, a ray of hope pierced through the darkness, reminding him that redemption was possible and that his shattered spirit could be made whole once more.

In anguish, he prayed, "Cast me not away from your presence and take not your Holy Spirit from me. Restore to me the joy of your salvation and uphold me with a willing spirit." (Psalm 51:10-12). He begged for a spiritual operation that only God could conduct. He longed for a clean heart and a renewed spirit. His plea for restoration echoed the deepest desires of his soul. He cried out to the heavens, yearning for a divine intervention that would wash away the stains of his past and illuminate his path toward redemption.

With every breath, he prayed for a fresh start and a chance for his life to be rewritten. He longed for his soul to be restored (Psalm 23:2). His anguished cries pierced the silence of the night, reverberating through the empty spaces of his solitary chamber. Each word he uttered carried the weight of his remorse and the fervent hope for a second chance.

Christ sacrificed himself to offer humanity forgiveness and spiritual cleansing. And this is what David cried out for in Psalm 51. In my experience, I have found that in certain traumatic instances, spiritual healing is crucial for individuals to receive release or deliverance from their pressing situations. Christ's sacrifice serves as a powerful symbol of redemption and inspiration for those seeking spiritual healing.

Spiritual healing provides inner peace, enabling mankind to fully address their traumas and embark on a transformative journey of healing and growth. Through embracing this profound act of love, individuals can find strength and solace in their faith, thereby allowing them to embark on a transformative journey toward wholeness and restoration.

CHAPTER ELEVEN

Sexual shame refers to the deep spiritual, emotional, psychological, and sometimes physical damage caused by the misuse, abuse, or distortion of God's design for sexuality. It can result from experiences such as sexual abuse, assault, exploitation, addiction, promiscuity, trauma, or even the silence and shame surrounding one's sexual identity or history.

Whether it is caused by our own choices or inflicted by others, sexual shame touches the very core of who we are because sex, in its original design, is not just a physical act, but a deeply spiritual and relational one.

God created sexuality as a sacred expression of love, covenant, and unity, intended for safety, mutual honor, and intimacy within marriage. But when this gift is violated, whether through abuse, manipulation, lust, or trauma, it fractures something sacred. That fracture creates a ripple effect, distorting not only how we see ourselves, but also how we view love, intimacy, safety, and even God.

Sexual pain carries a weight that often exceeds language. Its wounds don't just reside in the body; they imprint themselves on the soul. Some of the symptoms include:

Shame – A constant feeling of being unclean, unworthy, or unlovable.

Identity Confusion – Struggling to understand who you are or to feel secure in your body and self-worth.

Emotional Numbness or Hyper-sensitivity – Either disconnecting completely from feelings or being easily triggered by small events.

Addiction or Self-Destructive Behavior – Seeking escape, affirmation, or relief through harmful coping mechanisms.

Fear of Intimacy – Difficulty trusting others, maintaining relationships, or accepting healthy love.

Spiritual Disconnection – Believing God is distant, disappointed, or disinterested in your pain.

These effects are not always visible; however, these outcomes often drive people into cycles of silence, secrecy, and further wounding, until the pain becomes unbearable or numbing becomes normalized. The absence of visible scars does not mean the soul has not been wounded. Furthermore, wounds left unhealed become breeding grounds for deeper strongholds.

The Unseen Weight of Sexual Shame

Though Charlie and King David stand on opposite sides of the spectrum, one a victim, the other an offender, their stories intersect at a deeply human place: shame. Charlie, a teenage boy silenced by the weight of sexual trauma, carried invisible wounds that penetrated far beyond the surface. His pain was buried beneath shame, confusion, and a distorted sense of worth. In contrast, David's shame was self-inflicted. As king, he used his power to take Bathsheba, a married woman, and orchestrated her husband's death to cover the sin. Yet, despite the difference in how their wounds were inflicted, both suffered spiritually, emotionally, and psychologically.

Whether you are on the receiving end of abuse like Charlie or the one responsible for causing harm like David, the fallout of sexual shame is real, and it always demands divine healing.

The Hidden Nature of Shame and Silence

For Charlie, silence became a survival mechanism. Like many male victims of sexual trauma, he internalized the belief that real men don't speak about their pain. That silence became a prison, reinforced by fear, guilt, and rejection.

Similarly, David attempted to hide his actions, burying the truth beneath lies and manipulation. His initial refusal to confront his sin led to a downward spiral that affected his household and spiritual life. In Psalm 32, David writes, *"When I kept silent, my bones wasted away... day and night Your hand was heavy upon me."*

One of the most painful aspects of sexual shame is the silence that surrounds it, especially for men. Society often teaches men to be strong, silent, and stoic, making it even harder for male survivors of sexual abuse or trauma to speak out. For both men and women, the stigma attached to sexual wounds can lead to isolation, self-loathing, and spiritual despair.

The Church, though called to be a place of refuge, has sometimes failed to speak openly about sexual trauma and healing. In many communities, this has created a culture of avoidance, leaving individuals to battle their pain alone. But God is not afraid of our wounds. In fact, Jesus specializes in healing what others overlook.

Silence, whether it stems from fear or pride, always deepens the wound. Both Charlie and David needed a moment of truth, a divine interruption that would bring what was hidden into the light.

The Turning Point: Confrontation and Surrender

Healing for Charlie began the moment he stopped running from the pain and invited God into the broken places. It was in his moment of surrender that transformation started to take root. In a similar way, David's healing began when the prophet Nathan confronted him with the truth. His mask shattered, and repentance poured out of his heart in Psalm 51: *"Create in me a clean heart, O God, and renew a right spirit within me."*

Though their paths were different, both men reached a moment where truth was no longer avoidable, and it was there that the healing process really began. Confrontation, whether self-initiated or divinely led, is often the doorway to restoration.

The Power of Divine Healing and Restoration

What medical professionals, therapy, or human wisdom alone can not fully reach, the Spirit of God is able to restore. For Charlie, the touch of Jesus met him in the trauma he couldn't articulate. The Redeemer whispered identity, love, and safety into a place that had only known violation and fear.

For David, God's mercy did not erase the consequences of his sin, but it did offer him forgiveness and restoration. Despite his failures, David went on to become a worshipper, a psalmist, and a man after God's own heart. Both stories remind us that God does not define us by what we've done or what's been done to us. He defines us by who we are in Him.

The Message: Healing Is for Everyone

Charlie's story speaks to the silent sufferers, the ones who carry pain in secret, afraid to be seen. David's story speaks to the repentant, the ones who know they've fallen short and long to be made whole again.

Together, these narratives form a powerful truth: **God heals the wounded and restores the wayward. He delivers the brokenhearted and redeems the fallen.** Whether trauma was thrust upon you or you bear the weight of your own choices, the invitation to healing is the same. **Psalm 147:3** *"He heals the brokenhearted and binds up their wounds."* **Psalm 34:18** *"The Lord is close to the brokenhearted and saves those who are crushed in spirit."* **2 Corinthians 5:17** *"If anyone is in Christ, he is a new creation. The old has passed away; behold, all things have become new."*

The good news of the Gospel is that no shame is beyond the reach of God's healing. Jesus came not only to forgive sin, but to restore what was lost, to bind up the brokenhearted, to set the captives free (Luke 4:18), and to make all things new (Revelation 21:5). God is not afraid of your pain. He is not repulsed by your past. He doesn't overlook your trauma. He draws near to the broken (Psalm 34:18), and He speaks healing where silence once reigned. Whether you are the one who was abused, the one who crossed a boundary, or someone who feels lost in confusion and shame, there is hope.

Sexual shame doesn't have to define your life. With God, broken things become beautiful things. Scars become testimonies. Silence becomes songs of freedom. The story doesn't end in shame; it ends in restoration. *"He gives beauty for ashes, the oil of joy for mourning, and the garment of praise for the spirit of heaviness..."* (Isaiah 61:3)

CHAPTER TWELVE

Christ offers more than survival; He offers abundant life. Charlie's life was radically transformed the moment he encountered the love and grace of Jesus Christ. The weight of guilt and shame that once crushed him was lifted, replaced with a sense of purpose and renewed identity.

Through Christ, he discovered not only healing, but meaning. Likewise, King David, after falling into sin, found restoration through sincere repentance and a desperate cry for cleansing. Both stories remind us that no matter the depth of our pain or failure, the love of Christ has the power to redeem, restore, and redefine our lives.

The traumatic events that once marked their lives were not the end of their stories. Through divine encounters with the Master, those wounds were not only acknowledged, but they were also healed. Their testimonies now stand as living proof of the transformative power of Jesus Christ, a reminder that no pain is beyond His reach and no story too broken to be redeemed.

As you face the complexities of life, its trials, wounds, and uncertainties, may Charlie and David's stories stir something within you. May you find hope in the possibility of your own spiritual encounter. May you discover renewal in the presence of the One who sees, knows, and heals.

If you're living in the shadow of fear, wrestling with the silent weight of sexual trauma, pain, rejection, or guilt, I want you to hear this: You are not alone, and you are not beyond healing. You are not defined by what happened to you. You are not the shame you carry, the silence you've kept, or the pain that pierced your soul.

When the weight feels unbearable, may you be reminded that God is nearby. May you find strength to endure, wisdom to seek help, and the courage to open your heart to the Healer.

No matter what hardships you face, whether rooted in trauma, grief, rejection, or fear, faith in God can be your anchor. In the storms of life, when doubt clouds your vision and uncertainty shakes your footing, His love remains steady.

If you find yourself struggling today, bound by pain, trauma, fear, or guilt, know that healing is not only possible but also promised through Jesus Christ. The Word declares, "He heals the brokenhearted and binds up their wounds" (Psalm 147:3). But healing often begins with taking a step, reaching out, surrendering, and allowing others to walk with you in the power of the Spirit.

Seek out a Spirit-filled, biblically grounded ministry, one that is equipped to walk with you through the process of supernatural healing and restoration. As James 5:16 urges, "Confess your faults one to another, and pray one for another, that you may be healed." God often uses the body of Christ as vessels of His comfort and power.

Do not suffer in silence. Jesus has already paid the price for your freedom, and He has appointed Spirit-led shepherds to help guide you into wholeness. "Where the Spirit of the Lord is, there is liberty" (2 Corinthians 3:17), and in that liberty, your healing begins."

As you come to the end of this book, my prayer is that this would mark a new beginning for you, not just the closing of pages, but the opening of your heart to true transformation. I urge you: don't carry your trauma another day. Do spiritual work.

Lean into the process. Exchange your pain for purpose and your trauma for triumph.

You are not meant to merely survive; you are destined to overcome. You are meant to be victorious! When you face your fears and invite the healing presence of Jesus Christ into the deepest places of your heart, the wounds of your past can become wells of strength, wisdom and resilience.

"He gives beauty for ashes, the oil of joy for mourning, and the garment of praise for the spirit of heaviness" (Isaiah 61:3). This is not just a promise; it is the inheritance of every child of God. Let His love write a new story, one where faith replaces fear, freedom replaces shame, and victory rises from the ruins.

FINAL WORDS

There are some aches and injuries the body carries that medicine cannot reach. While doctors can diagnose, treat, and even save lives through their God-given knowledge and compassion, there are damaged places in the soul that only the hand of the Divine can mend.

To medical professionals, your work is special. Your wisdom, your care, your knowledge, and skillful hands have brought healing and relief into the lives of countless people. For that, we are deeply grateful. Your commitment to healing reflects the very heart of our Creator, who equips and anoints people like you to bring consolation in times of chaos.

But for the wound's unseen, the unspoken injuries, the pain that haunts the mind and soul long after the body has healed, there is a Healer whose power knows no bounds. His name is Jesus Christ.

I've learned that true healing is not merely the absence of pain, but the presence of peace. Deliverance isn't just freedom from torment; it's the restoration of identity, dignity, and purpose. And freedom, real, lasting freedom, is found only in the One who bled and died, then rose again to give us new life.

I know what trauma can do. I've felt its grip tighten around my soul, and I've walked through the suffocating shadows it casts. I've been caught in the web of its lies and entangled in the pain it leaves behind. But I have also encountered something greater, the unmatched power of God to heal, deliver, and set the captives free. What no therapist could fully explain, what no medication could quiet, the Spirit of the Living God confronted and dismantled. He met me in the depths with truth that pierced through the darkness, love that restored what was broken and resurrection power that brought me back to life.

"Whom the Son sets free is free indeed" (John 8:36). These are not just words; they are the anthem of my life. So, if you find yourself still in the valley, know this: you are not alone. There is hope. There is healing. And there is a God who sees you, loves you, and will stop at nothing to restore you.

The grace of God is still healing hearts today, and it's available to *you*, right now. No matter how deep the emotional injury or how long the pain has lingered, God's healing power reaches beyond time, trauma, and circumstance as you reflect on the message of **When Trauma Writes the Story: Triumph Wins!** *"From Brokenness to Beauty"*, my heartfelt hope is that you, too, will experience the breakthrough you've been longing for. Healing is not just a distant possibility; it is a present invitation.

These may be my final words, but for you, they mark the beginning of a new chapter. A chapter not defined by pain, but by promise. Not shaped by trauma but transformed by truth. Jesus declared, *"The Spirit of the Lord is upon me, because he has anointed me to proclaim good news to the poor. He has sent me to bind up the brokenhearted, to proclaim freedom for the captives and release from darkness for the prisoners."* Isaiah 61:1 (NIV)

So now, it's your turn. **Step forward. Seek healing. Embrace freedom.** And with open hands and a surrendered heart, **let the Healer write the rest of your story.**

If you're ready to take that first courageous step toward wholeness, I invite you to pause and pray the prayer below. Let this be more than just words on a page. Let it be a sacred moment of encounter, a divine intersection where heaven meets your pain, and Jesus begins to write a new chapter of healing, redemption, freedom, and triumph in your life.

PRAYER

Heavenly Father,

I come before You today with an open heart, tired,
wounded, but ready.
Ready to believe that You are the God who heals,
restores, and redeems.
You know the pain I've carried, the trauma I've endured, and
the pieces of myself I've tried to hold together.
I can't hide it from You, and I'm tired pretending
I just can't do it anymore.

Lord, I lay it all at Your feet. The memories I can't escape.

The voices of guilt and shame that echo in my mind.
The fear that paralyzes me.
The rejection that still stings.
The silence that has shouted louder than words ever could.

Today, I choose to believe that I don't have to stay broken. I
believe that Your grace is big enough for me, and Your love is
strong enough to reach the deepest places of my pain.

Jesus, I invite You into every hidden corner of my heart. Touch
the parts of me that still bleed. Heal the wounds that still bleed,
that I'm tired of ignoring. Heal what I cannot fix.
I believe You died for my sins and to make me whole.

Restore to me what was stolen. Redeem what was lost.
Rewrite my story with Your hand of mercy and make triumph
the final chapter.

FROM BROKENNESS TO BEAUTY
I want to be free!

Today, I take the first step. I receive Your love.
I receive Your healing.

And I declare, by faith, that my story is not over
Because with You, Jesus, I will overcome.

In Your powerful and healing name,
Amen.

ENCOURAGEMENT

To every man reading this who has carried the silent weight of
sexual abuse, ***please hear this:***
You are not weak because you were wounded.
You are not broken beyond repair.
And you are not alone.

What was done to you does not define who you are.

You are worthy of healing.
You are worthy of love.
You are worthy of peace.

There is no shame in your story, only strength in your survival
and even greater strength in your surrender to the One who
heals.

Jesus sees you. He believes you.
And He has not forgotten you.

Your voice matters. Your healing matters.
You matter. This is not the end.
It's the beginning.
And with Christ, you will rise.

FROM BROKENNESS TO BEAUTY
DECLARATIONS OF HEALING AND IDENTITY

Speak these truths aloud over your life. Let the Word of God reframe your thoughts, restore your identity, and rebuild what trauma tried to tear down.

1. I am not what happened to me: I am who God says I am. *"Therefore, if anyone is in Christ, he is a new creation; the old has gone, the new has come."* - 2 Corinthians 5:17 (NIV)

2. I am not defined by my past: I am redeemed by grace. *"In Him we have redemption through His blood, the forgiveness of sins, in accordance with the riches of God's grace."* - Ephesians 1:7 (NIV)

3. I am not alone: God is with me in every battle. *"Be strong and courageous. Do not be afraid; do not be discouraged, for the Lord your God will be with you wherever you go."* - Joshua 1:9 (NIV)

4. I am not powerless: I have authority through Christ. *"I have given you authority... to overcome all the power of the enemy; nothing will harm you."* - Luke 10:19 (NIV)

5. I am healed: spirit, soul, and body. *"He heals the brokenhearted and binds up their wounds."* - Psalm 147:3 (NIV). *"By His wounds we are healed."* - Isaiah 53:5 (NIV)

6. I am a man/woman of purpose, strength, and dignity. *"The Lord is my strength and my shield; my heart trusts in Him, and He helps me."* - Psalm 28:7 (NIV)

7. I am rising from the ruins. My story is not over. *"The Lord will restore the years the locusts have eaten."* Joel 2:25 (NIV). *"Weeping may last through the night, but joy comes in the* *morning."* - Psalm 30:5 (NLT)

8. I am chosen, loved, and never forsaken.
"You did not choose me, but I chose you." - John 15:16 (NIV)
"I will never leave you nor forsake you." - Hebrews 13:5 (NIV)

I declare today that I will no longer live
in the shadow of shame.

I will walk in truth, healing, and freedom.

I am a son of the Most High God.

I am whole. I am free. In Jesus' name, Amen.

ABOUT THE AUTHOR:

Dr. Kayla Bullard: A Trailblazer in Transformative Education and Innovation

Dr. Kayla Bullard is a dynamic leader and visionary in the field of education, celebrated for her unwavering commitment to empowering learners and educators through innovation and inclusion. Born with an insatiable curiosity and a deep passion for reading, Dr. Bullard has devoted her life to reshaping traditional approaches to education, ensuring that every individual has the opportunity to unlock their full potential.

With an impressive academic foundation, Dr. Bullard earned her Ph.D. in Educational Leadership from Texas Christian University, a prestigious institution. Throughout her career, Dr. Bullard has held numerous leadership positions, ranging from classroom educator to school administrator, and now serves as a sought-after educational leader, consultant, and speaker. Her innovative approach has transformed computer education and teacher training, fostering creativity, critical thinking, and collaboration in schools in Freeport, Grand Bahama, Georgia, Nebraska, and Texas. Dr. Bullard has been featured as a trendsetter in her native country as a trailblazer in computer education, where she has shared her expertise on topics such as digital literacy, culturally responsive teaching, and the future of education.

Beyond her professional achievements, Dr. Bullard is known for her genuine warmth and ability to connect with people from all walks of life. Her collaborative approach has inspired countless educators to embrace change and champion the needs of their students. She also dedicates time to mentoring emerging leaders in education, ensuring the next generation continues to innovate and advocate for equitable learning opportunities.

When she's not transforming educational landscapes, Dr. Bullard enjoys traveling, exploring diverse cultures, and volunteering in community development initiatives. Her life's work is a testament to her belief that education is the cornerstone of progress, and her legacy continues to inspire educators and learners alike to dream bigger, aim higher, and never stop growing.

Her passion for transformation extends beyond education into storytelling. From Brokenness to Beauty is the fourth installment in her powerful series, When Trauma Writes the Story Triumph Wins! —a collection that seeks to bring healing and hope through testimony, faith, and transformation.

Connect with Dr. Kayla Bullard and join the movement toward healing and triumph! drkayla.bullard@gmail.com